"*It's* All Good"

"*It's* All Good"

A Grieving Mother's Journal

JULIA WATSON

"IT'S ALL GOOD"
A GRIEVING MOTHER'S JOURNAL

iUniverse books may be ordered through booksellers or by contacting:

iUniverse
1663 Liberty Drive
Bloomington, IN 47403
www.iuniverse.com
1-800-Authors (1-800-288-4677)

ISBN: 978-1-4917-4906-7 (sc)
ISBN: 978-1-4917-4907-4 (e)

Library of Congress Control Number: 2014917772

Printed in the United States of America.

iUniverse rev. date: 10/14/2014

For

Sarah

Jake

Tom

Marilyn

*A special thank you to Ed
for never giving up.*

Dedicated in loving memory to
Amy Katherine Burgess Reynolds

Acknowledgments

I would like to personally acknowledge two friends who, throughout this journey, always knew exactly what to say and what to do at exactly the right time. Thank you so much

Sally Ham
and
Beth Kiel

Contents

Preface xi

Chapter 1   2010-The beginning or the end?............................1

Chapter 2   2011-They say it gets easier after the first year 25

Chapter 3   2012-They lied...43

Chapter 4   2013-The definition of insanity...........................53

Chapter 5   2014-Voices 62

Epilogue   Amy's Christmas Note..73

Preface

My grandfather wrote poetry, my daughter secretly writes romance novels and my brother is a published author. I always believed they were the written communicators in our family. They have a unique ability to provide readers with eloquent words of inspiration or to create a story line so captivating you can visualize it in your mind. They were the authors. I sat on the sidelines and was their biggest fan.

I was comfortable with that role and believed it was where I belonged. That, however, changed in 2010 when I was thrown into a world of darkness and solitude. It was almost three months after the death of my daughter Amy that I realized I had no voice. I could not speak the words that churned inside my heart and soul. I didn't have the ability to verbalize or express my irrational or rational thoughts, my struggles, my heartache, my anger, my disbelief, my guilt or my belief in the God I thought I knew. My entire being became festered and infected, ready to boil over.

The inner turmoil and pressure building inside me had to find a release from somewhere or the explosion would take me down a path that I knew I could never recover. I was forced to write; I had to. There simply was no option. For almost four years, I spewed out everything I thought, saw, felt or heard into a journal entitled *"A Grieving Mother's Journal"*. I didn't care who or if anyone read it. I didn't care how it sounded. I certainly didn't worry about punctuation, spelling or grammar. Whatever flew out of my heart and head went straight to my fingers and a keyboard. I found my voice and a sounding board in an electronic device.

In July, 2014, my journal was completed and my voice returned. Those days of speaking only through a silent medium was replaced by an overwhelming desire to say and do more. I was summoned by a power beyond myself to share this journey, hoping it would bring relief, comfort and a renewed spirit to others. My prayer is that something in this book brings peace and reassurance, even if the only thing anyone remembers is, *"It's all good".*

Chapter 1

2010-The beginning or the end?

"Several years later I divorced, had a whirl-wind romance and remarried"

I grew up in a small town in western Kentucky. My household included my father, mother, brother and grandmother. I guess at that time we were considered upper middle class. Both parents worked in public businesses and reputation played an important role in their lives. Along with reputation came certain expectations. One included attending church. Almost every weekend we put on our Sunday best, were told to spit out our gum before entering the building, and then we made our way up the steps and into the Methodist Church.

I was christened as an infant in that church as were most of my friends who also attended. When we were twelve, our Sunday school class met with the pastor for instructions on baptism. Even now I have no clue what he said except that we had a choice to be "sprinkled" or "immersed". On that eventful day, my classmates and I were "invited" down to the altar. We were asked a couple of questions (can't remember what they were) and we obediently recited the script that had been given us during our training. Once everything was said, we all knelt down, bowed our heads and the pastor went from person to person placing his water-filled hands on our washed, dried and curled hair.

That was how I became a Christian. (This is where you chuckle)

There was always something stirring in me and even on that baptism Sunday, I wanted more. Although we went to church regularly, we never discussed God, Jesus or religion. My mother kept The Upper Room in the bathroom and read it while doing her business. Occasionally, during holidays and family reunions, someone would say the blessing. So what I learned was the story of The Ten Commandments and Moses, a little about Jonah, the birth of Christ (that was Christmas), his death and his resurrection (that was Easter) along with some great old hymns. I struggled with right and wrong. One day I was going to the elderly neighbors across the street and cleaning their house and the next day I was looking for any unacceptable and exciting adventure I could find.

As everyone knows, the older you get, the more risky those adventures become. I ran off and got married the day after I graduated from high school. Life during the '60's and early '70's was a challenge for every restless young adult, not just me. There were assassinations and riots; rallying cries for love, peace, and the end of war. No one was very far removed from parties and illegal drugs. For me, it was an internal battle between conforming to what I had been taught and believed to rebelling against everything my parents and the establishment stood for.

But nothing changes you more than having children. It was the only definite thing I ever wanted. I adored my two daughters and knew they were a blessing from God. I joined a church and became an active member. My girls were christened. It was a smart (or maybe something else) thing to do because one weekend after reading a book someone from that church had given me, my internal struggle with right and wrong ended. I discovered that always trying to figure it out, always waiting for the big lightning bolt or always beating myself up for not being a better person was all backwards. It was much simpler than that. All I had to do was stop and accept that God loves me. His willingness to forgive is so much greater than any wrong I can ever do. When I simply lifted my head and gave myself completely to Him, I was filled with a joy and contentment I had never known. If you're a Christian, you know it's called the Holy Spirit.

That was how I became a Christian the second time. (This is where you grin and nod yes)

Several years later, I divorced, had a whirl-wind romance and remarried. This marriage came with all the odds of never making it past one year. Bitter step-children, thousands of dollars in debt, loss of job, moving out of state, moving again and moving again, children living with us and then moving out, children's reckless and self-destructive behavior, husband's parents dying, loss of job and then, of all things, moving back to the city and state where it all began. Did I mention that at one point I left my husband? He always had a "cause" that consumed him and most of the time it was at the expense of his family. The separation didn't last long but was enough for me to question everything. My marriage was unstable and the outlook for us having a loving home and family was bleak.

We bought a house and settled in. It was nice to be back with familiarity and good friends. I became my mother's caretaker, had a job I loved and became a grandmother for the first time. Our marriage was still rocky but we really looked like the perfect couple in public. My husband was so very unhappy. He hated his job, thought constantly about how to make more money and had some grandiose idea of becoming a super star in his marketing company. I got so tired of just hoping for the opportunity to once again be an important part of his life. That happened in the year 2001.

We made plans to dine at a nice restaurant to celebrate our anniversary. While we were there, I could tell Ed was fidgety and nervous. I thought he had lost his job, wanted to move again or was needing to end our marriage. This is a summary of what he told me. He had been to the doctor for the first time in years. They ran some tests and he was told to go home, get his affairs in order and be at the hospital Monday morning for a heart cath. I didn't understand the impact of what the doctor had said to him. I just assumed we would go Monday, have whatever it was fixed, leave with a couple of prescriptions and then go back to our normal lives. There was a family event in Louisville that weekend I was going to cancel but did not due to my husband's insistence. He said he just needed time to be alone. I considered it another wedge in our relationship. You know what else will change you other than having children? Looking at your death straight in the eye. That's what happened to Ed on that weekend in April, 2001.

Ed and I, along with two of his children, went to the hospital for his "procedure". Over the years, I have learned to hate that word. While in the waiting room, we watched doctors come and talk to family members. They would breathe a sigh of relief, say thanks to the doctor and then go get coffee and/or a cigarette. We waited and waited until finally someone came to us and said we needed to follow them to a back room. The doctor wanted to speak to us. Over the years, I have also learned to hate it when they want to take you to a room so the doctor can speak to you. Totally unaware of what was happening, we trudged back and heard the doctor tell us Ed had to have emergency by-pass surgery. We could go in and see him for a couple of minutes and then they needed to get him prepped immediately for surgery. As strange as it may sound, when I entered that room and Ed held out his hand and wanted me by his side, I knew how much we loved each other and all the other stuff in our lives was totally insignificant.

We changed in different ways after that. Ed's spiritually soared and he considered his surgery a gift from God. I considered it a pain in my ass. I never knew if his aches and pains were normal or a sign of trouble. I was afraid of giving him the wrong medicine or the wrong dosage at the wrong time. Trying to figure out a heart healthy diet after years of cooking meat and potatoes in bacon grease was enough to send me over the edge. It was a full year before I could even say he had almost completely recovered. But he did recover and we went about our new lives that included a chance (or maybe something else) meeting with a pastor named Silas. We followed and learned from him and our faith was once again renewed. We joined the church, became active members and witnessed how family members struggling with cancer faced adversity. We met some of the most wonderful people we've ever known and they are still part of our lives today. God was good. He had been there in Ed's hour of need and led us to a place where we could grow spiritually, slowly and steadily. Our marriage was being put back together piece by piece, day by day.

In 2006, my mother died at the age of eighty-eight. Ed retired, my job had become more of a headache than a pleasure and my two daughters lived in Indianapolis. My daughter, Sarah, recently divorced and raising her son Jake, had been begging us to move up there. She was going to school full time and worked at the Heart Center on the weekends. She could use our help. Sarah had purchased a large home with four bedrooms, three baths and a huge yard, so there would be plenty of room. With her insistence (or maybe it was something else), we decided, why not? We could stay a year, help out and if we didn't like it or it didn't work out, we could always move back. Ed's retirement check could go with us anywhere we went.

We did move to Indy and began going to a church where my oldest daughter, Amy, and her husband attended. Sarah would go occasionally and it was at that church where Jake was baptized. We celebrated that event with cake, ice cream, family and friends and once again were reminded that God is good. And then it happened again. In 2007, Ed had issues and was told he needed another heart by-pass.

That's when I really started believing that God had set things in motion years before we had any inkling of what was going to happen. How is it that before Ed's first heart surgery, we just suddenly decided to quit smoking? How did the timing of my mother's death, Ed's retirement and dissatisfaction with my job lead to the opportunity of moving to a place that has the best medical care in the nation? Hospitals and doctors weren't anywhere in our decision to move. How did it happen that my daughter was working at a heart hospital when it could easily have been any other hospital in that huge city? Because she worked there, she knew who was the best cardiologist and heart surgeon and was aware of what was happening and when. Her experience and insight helped us determine choices we would never have understood or made. Ed did have his second by-pass surgery and it went well. His recovery was much faster than before. I believed and my faith grew.

We eventually decided to hang around Indianapolis for a little longer. We moved to an apartment and Sarah sold her big house and bought a more manageable one. Jake was our center and a constant joy. There were several trips with Ed to the Heart Center for stents, but considering everything, we were doing well. We enjoyed the company of my daughters and it didn't take long for them to become "our" daughters. The special bond between those three is something I couldn't explain (or maybe it was something else) but it made my heart sing. We all took vacations and road trips together. Discussions and topics of the day were often spent around the table playing rook or dominos. Amy and Ed were involved in the church and spent many hours discussing and planning events. And then, yes, again, in 2008 we were faced with a third open heart surgery.

Ed was back at the Heart Center and his cardiologist was a little unnerved with the prospects of a third surgery. She wasn't the only one. Ed had to make a decision whether or not to even have the surgery. While in the hospital his cardiologist was determined to have only the best surgeon. She absolutely refused to let anyone else touch him. While waiting to set something up with the surgeon, they wanted to put Ed on a heart pump. Sarah was adamant that they not do that. She said there were too many complications involved with that "procedure". The heart surgeon we insisted on having told us he was so booked that it would be at least a minimum of three days before he could schedule Ed's surgery. It was terrible. Obviously, the cardiologist was concerned that if Ed didn't have this surgery soon, he could have a nasty heart attack. We also knew the longer the wait, the less likely he would agree to have the surgery and no one liked the outcome that would present.

It was early the next morning when a nurse came in and said they needed to prep Ed for surgery. What? How? Who? What are you talking about? And there it was; "There was a cancellation this morning and the surgeon is available now". No one cancels heart surgery. It had to be a God thing. I knew it. God was moving obstacles out of the way and once again taking care of us. I believed and my faith grew. Ed recovered and everyone in the medical community still considers anyone who survives three open heart surgeries a walking miracle (or maybe it was something else). For two years we enjoyed the day-to-day ups and downs that everyday life brings. We went to church, I got a part time job, and we grew as a family knowing God had brought us through some of the scariest and hardest times in our lives. We were going to be ok.

On June 9, 2008, I began writing a "praise" journal. Every night before I went to sleep, I would always try to write something positive about the day and end it with a Bible verse. It was a way for me to try, and I must admit sometimes it wasn't easy, to find something good about the day and to thank God for those moments.

Here are some randomly selected samples:

Four days after Ed's open heart surgery. For Ed, the Lord gave me this verse-Psalm 20.

Ed home from hospital. Saw a cardinal, blue jay and robin at our feeder-1 Cor: 15

Amy's car broke down & we help. Sarah helps provide medical care and reassurance. Amy and Dean provide company. We help with Jake. We all help each other over and over and over-Ecclesiastes 4: 9-12

Dinner and movie with Jake. I pray he remembers me as a child of God, just like him-1 John 3:7

Death of a friend. What a blessing for me to have known you. I will miss you. You inspired so many people and showed us what true courage is-Matthew 6:25-34

Marilyn got a job! She and Tom have no idea how many prayers have been lifted up for them. "Therefore encourage one another and build each other up." Praises to God for answering this one.

July 20, 2010 (PET scan) "Though you have made me see troubles, many and bitter, you will restore my life again; from the depths of the earth you will again bring me up. You will increase my honor and comfort me once again." Psalm

71:20-21. "Then Job replied to the Lord; 'I know that you can do all things; no plan of yours can be thwarted' Job 42:1

Chemo/hospital/sick

I can't... not now.

I have to stop. God has to work around me, over me and through me. I have moved, but I am certain – He has not.

That was my last *"praise"* entry in this journal.

Owensboro, KY Obituary

Amy K. (Burgess) Reynolds, 39, passed away on September 22, 2010, after a brief battle with cancer.

She is survived by her loving husband, Dean; mother Julie (Sis) Watson (Ed); father Ronnie Burgess (Jacquie); grandmother Jean Burgess Ashby; sister Sarah Small; nephew Jake Small; uncles Tom Wallace(Marilyn) and Mark Burgess(Elizabeth) and aunts Janet Durall(Bill) and Linda Reid(Jimmy); step-brothers Byron Watson(Mary) & Mark Watson(Libby); and step-sister Cindy Caldwell(Mike). Amy was preceded in death by her grandparents Fred & Louise Wallace and Bill Burgess.

Amy was a graduate of Apollo High School, Owensboro, KY, and continued her study of music and vocal performance in college. Amy was certified as a pharmacy technician in the state of Indiana in 2007, and was most recently employed as an administrative assistant at Eli Lilly & Company. She has worked as a Director/Minister of Arts & Music at multiple churches in the Indianapolis area and loved lending her talents to praise and honor God.

Amy had a great passion for local community theatre and made a lasting contribution to this community. She was a talented vocalist; vocal director; conductor; vocal coach; pianist and piano teacher; accompanist; actor and has been honored for her talents by the local community theatre association.

Amy was blessed with a great sense of humor; an infectious smile; an adventurous spirit; boundless energy; remarkable creativity and a positive outlook on life.

Amy treasured the time spent with her family and she expanded her definition of family to include her friends. Some of her most enjoyable family time was spent playing the piano and singing after family dinners. Probably her favorite family time of all was her "Aunt Wheeza Days" spent with her nephew Jake.

She will be deeply missed by all her family and friends and we join in saying "because we knew you, we have been changed for good".

It was the Fourth of July, 2010, with everyone at our house for grilling, eating and games. It was one of those laid-back days that makes you appreciate the holiday and that extra day off work. Amy had been seeing a chiropractor for several weeks due to some back pain. This was rare for Amy. Seldom sick and always considered strong as a mule, it was unusual for her to talk about her back hurting. As things were winding down, we all sat around talking about everything and nothing. Amy stretched out on the couch with her head in my lap and I, as I always did, unconsciously began tickling and rubbing her back. I felt a lump in her lower back. Our conversation bounced back and forth between us in such a carefree easy way. I can still recall, word for word what was spoken during that holiday gathering.

"Amy, what's that".

"Oh, the chiropractor said it's a lipoma".

"No it's not. I've felt lipomas before and this doesn't feel like one. Sarah, come and check this out".

"Amy, I don't think it is".

"Well, I don't know, but it sure does hurt".

"Why don't you go to a medical doctor and find out?"

"I work tomorrow and it's really hurting, so I think I'll go to the emergency room and see if they can do something for me. Sarah, want to go with me?"

"Sure, let me get my purse."

Julia Watson

Excerpts from "A Grieving Mother's Journal"

So, she and Sarah drove off with us believing that Amy probably had a disc problem or pinched nerve. After all, bad backs run in our family. Never, ever did any thoughts of what was about to transpire enter into my mind. No one was prepared for the news my daughters brought with them when they returned from the hospital. X-rays showed swollen lymph nodes in the back and stomach. Blood tests showed no sign of infection. According to the doctor, there was only one conclusion. You know, I don't remember anyone ever using the word cancer that day, at least not to me. It was simply stated in a way that made it clear that whatever it was; it was not going to be good.

It began. A call to the doctor and an immediate appointment with the oncologist. Lymph nodes in the stomach, back and clavicle area swollen from the cancer. He was pretty certain the source was somewhere in the stomach area, but unsure. They would need to do a few more tests and a colonoscopy. In the meantime, they would start her on a chemo regimen. My God how fast things were moving. How could we even digest all that was happening and questions we couldn't or even know how to ask? I went with Amy to almost every appointment. I was working part time in the cafeteria of an elementary school and explained that I needed to be off on Amy's "bad" days. I wanted to be there to hold her head while vomiting and there to clean the toilet and bring her food. I had to find a way to comfort her and mother her and take care of her. I remember going with her to the first chemo treatment. While we sat in the waiting room I looked around at all the elderly patients and thought, *how can it be that we're here? Amy's young and strong. It's ok though, we'll get through this and after treatments and recuperation, my daughter and all of us will be fine. God has pulled us through a lot of rough times and I know He'll do it again.* They put in a port to help make getting treatments and drawing blood easier. Amy was finally able to have the colonoscopy and the diagnosis was colon cancer.

Excerpts from "Amy's Background Story". CaringBridge, a website set up for Amy

2010

August 13th:

Now that I have met with the oncologist and we have a plan, I thought I would give a quick update for everyone who hasn't been in the immediate loop this week.

As we know, the primary site of my cancer is colon. They found a 2cm flat lesion on the left upper side of the colon in front of the liver. It is small and extremely treatable. First, there will be no surgery or radiation. It isn't necessary for the size and shape. So praise God for that. Second, the chemo regimen will be every 2 weeks for about 24 weeks. That time may vary depending on how well my body responds to the drugs. The chemo and the iron (to help with the anemia) infusion will take about 5 hours each time.

The side effects are pretty normal, but a little less toxic than the first round that I had a couple of Fridays ago. Hair loss, fatigue, sick tummy, some blood count issues and then of course the weakened immune system. The doctor says that this combination of drugs has an extremely high success rate and has no doubt that it shouldn't work just as successfully for me.

I am looking forward to seeing how my body handles everything so I know when my good days and bad days will be. Plus after this first couple of rounds, I should be able to get off of the pain drip. That will be a happy day.

I am so thankful for all of the family and friends who are supporting me. We have a long road ahead but I know I have so much love around me that the road will be so much easier. And I look forward to start sending updates about how much of the cancer is gone and the progress we are making!

Love to you all,

Amy

Julia Watson

Amy's outlook was positive and she continued singing with the praise and worship team at church. The pastor and many of the congregation prayed for her and they even surrounded her with prayer and "laid hands" on her. There were people in the Carolinas, Kentucky, Tennessee, as well as Indiana, on their knees praying. But once the chemo started, it was ugly from the beginning. Constant vomiting and dry heaves; pain meds, pain pump, hair loss; multiple trips to the hospital for dehydration and anemia; ninety pounds down in a month, a clogged port and only an occasional good day. Finally, it was the last trip to the hospital. The only way I can describe Amy's dying was like this: the cancer was now in her bloodstream and going to the brain. While in the hospital she complained of a headache and asked me for a Tylenol. I laughed, saying with all the pain meds in you, I doubt if a Tylenol will help. Little did I know what was happening inside her body. Throughout this entire ordeal, Amy never really complained. I/we should have known something significant was going on. But how could we?

This last conscious event of her life happened within a twenty four hour period. There was swelling around the brain. What transpired in her appearance and actions were unbearable to watch. It was the most horrible sight I have ever or ever will witness. They gave her enough medication to keep her still and quiet so they could run tests and x-rays. No one was sure why her condition had turned so critical, so fast. Because of so much medication and her deteriorating condition, she had to be placed on a ventilator and they put in a central line. It didn't take but a couple of days before the doctors decided to do an EEG. The next day we were at her bedside when the doctor came in and asked us to go into a private room so he could speak with us. I knew. No cognitive brain activity. No possibility of her being more than what she was in that hospital bed. A decision had to be made to take her off the ventilator and let nature/God take its course. No more chemo treatments. No more remission. No more recuperation. No cure. It was over. We decided to take her off the ventilator the following day. They would take out the ventilator, clean her up, move her to a private room, attach a pain pump and blood pressure monitor and give us the privacy needed during this horrific time. I remember we went home the night before she was to be taken off the ventilator. I don't remember sleeping. As I dressed the following morning to go back to the hospital, I looked at Ed and said *"This is the day my daughter is going to die".*

It was around three months after Amy died that I started journaling again and it definitely wasn't a *"praise"* journal. I also wrote some intimate letters addressed only to her. I have included a lot of my writings so everyone can see where I've been and how far I've come. My prayer is that whoever continues on this journey with me until the end will be comforted or at least find a glimmer of hope. This is a small piece of God's story written through me for any grieving parent or unbelieving person.

Amy was thirty nine when she died. Prior to her death, we had been giving her a hard time about turning forty but as it turned out, she was eighty-one days shy of that birthday.

From "My Birthday Letter to Amy"

December 12, 2010

Forty years ago, I was twenty one. I was too naive and green around the gills to know how to have a child, much less raise one. The only thing I knew for sure was how desperately I wanted you. Excited, terrified and unclear of how it all works, on Saturday, December 12, 1970 at 3:35 a.m., they placed you in my arms and I knew my life would never be the same. I didn't know how we were going to make it, I just knew we would. And in spite of all obstacles, for forty years, we did.

You were the first. You were the first child, the first grandchild and the first great-grandchild. I remember one time when you were a baby; someone looked at you and told me they thought you were as beautiful as any doll they had ever seen. All I could do was just say, "Yes, I know. She is beautiful, isn't she?" When Sarah was born I stayed in the hospital six days. I remember when they brought you to visit, I started to cry. You looked so grown up (you were 2 ½). You had on the cutest yellow and white dress, lace trimmed socks and your hair was so shiny. I wondered how you would like having a little sister and if it would make you sad or upset. You became a true blessing to your wonderful baby sister and you never complained.

I remember the first time you sang in public. It was in Owensboro at Wesleyan Heights UMC. I can't remember the choir director's name. You know who I'm talking about. Tall, bald, pretty music savvy for a choir director. I'll think of it in the middle of the night. Anyway, it was a Christmas program and you were playing the part of Mary. I think you were only five or six years old at the time. You had a solo and I was about to have a nervous breakdown when it was your turn to sing. (Little did I know I would do that every time you sang) Of course, you pulled it off magnificently. It wasn't too many years after that when Pat Schmied said she wanted to set up an appointment with you, me and Dr. Robert McIver who worked at Kentucky Wesleyan College. Pat told me she thought Doc would be very interested in hearing you sing. I laughed and said I knew you could carry a tune, but why on earth would a professor of music at the college want to hear my daughter sing? Speaking of naïve and green around the gills! McIver listened to you, came out of the music room and told me he never taught kids as young as you, but wanted to work and train with you immediately. I was stunned. I was also broke and told him I didn't have money for lessons. He didn't care. He said he would do it for free and it was at that time, I knew you had something very special.

Your gift of music isn't the only thing special you possess. You have an internal strength so many of your Indiana friends don't even know about. You have taken all aspects of your life, good and bad, and turned them inside out and upside down to become the wonderful, amazing adult you are now. I give all the credit to you. You are an inspiration to me, your mother, and the one who should inspire you. Funny how sometimes things get turned around.

You were admitted into the hospital with a severe infection at five weeks old; later, it was a broken arm; a split head needing eight stitches; a thumb that was caught in a steel door tearing off your nail and chipping the end of the bone also requiring stitches; a broken ankle and several sprains; and, of course, the infamous trip to the hospital from your tonsillectomy where you ended up having to have three units of blood and almost dying. No matter what it was, you always pulled through. That's why when I was told you had cancer, I truly believed it was just another hurdle you would jump through and, as usual, come out bigger and better. I didn't bury my head in the sand. I knew it was going to be a battle, but I also knew you would be in remission by the first of the year (2011), and we would have many months and maybe years left with you. Never in my mind or heart was I prepared to have it any other way. You always came through. How could you not, especially now? You are a strong, courageous, deliberate, healthy, positive, passionate woman who is needed and loved by so many. How could you not win this fight? From the age of five weeks until September 2010, you have always defied the odds. I've seen it so many times before and my heart simply refuses to believe differently.

So, right now, you are here. I know how really deep inside, you're not thrilled with being 40. I also know you're very tolerant and gracefully allow us the opportunity to poke fun at you with your reader glasses and shades of grey hair. I know you're glad everyone is here to celebrate your birthday. I also know whatever your age, you will never stop that inquisitive, little girl inside you who loves life and loves people and loves fun and loves her family and loves her friends and loves music and loves adventure and really does love big.

My arms are wrapped around you and with extreme pride and so much love; I wish you a very happy 40th birthday.

Mom

From "My Christmas Letter to Amy"

December 26, 2010

Well, Amy, the Christmas decorations have been taken down and stored in the garage for another year.

We did what was expected from us. First came the shopping, then wrapping the presents, decorating the tree, baking goodies and delivering to neighbors and hanging garland on the mantle with the red candles and bows. Next was the Owensboro Christmas. Then back home for the Indianapolis Christmas. The cards we received were from family and friends wishing us happy holidays along with handwritten notes stating their condolences and heartfelt prayers. All saying how much they knew this Christmas would be difficult for us. If they only knew. Difficult doesn't even come close.

It was all so fake. The holiday season just magnified the pain and emptiness I feel from your absence. There wasn't a song, decoration, wrapping paper, bow, ribbon, candy or cookie that didn't remind me of you. I played the Christmas video of you and closed my eyes, hoping against hope you were in the next room singing. Or sometimes, I simply touched the screen trying, once again, to feel your skin on my fingers. There has been no joy in this season of what once was my favorite time of the year. There were no lights or Santas or carols that made this Christmas anything but pure torture for me. My grief has only grown and even though I thought I had come to grips with you being gone, the realization is really only beginning. That was the cruelest gift I received during this holiday season.

I did the Christmas thing. We all did. We did it for you and hopefully, in some way, we honored you. You're the only person that could make what we went through worth it. I love you, Amy and I miss you. Because I love you so much, I will dredge up these words just for you,

Merry Christmas

Mom

Chapter 2

2011-They say it gets easier after the first year

*"We took a family photo and when I looked
at it there was a glaring absence."*

Julia Watson

Excerpts from "A Grieving Mother's Journal"

January, 2011 (3 months after Amy's death)

It's not necessary to almost die in order to have an out of body experience. Just bury your daughter. Yes, you feel the pain and you cry and you know what's happening around you, but it's like you're talking about someone else or doing things someone else would do. In an odd way, you can almost distance yourself. You can say her name and talk about things, but it's just words and actions. Then, after it's over and the weeks turn into months, instead of time healing; the wounds become more festered, raw and infected. It all becomes very real for you. Not someone else. But you.

Excerpts from "A Grieving Mother's Journal"

January, 2011

Somewhere inside your brain, you know so many of your thought processes are not rational. You honestly think you're going insane. You're jealous of all cancer survivors. Who gives a damn about pink ribbons? So they're getting closer to new cancer drugs that may cure or delay death. Whoopee. Too late. Don't care. Where have your friends and relatives gone? Were they ever here before she died? Are they staying away because of your child's death or have you shut them out to the extent they've stopped trying? I want to talk about her. I want to tell you the details of her life and what an incredible person she was. I want to tell you how we found out she had cancer and what happened in the last 81 days of her life. That's how long it took. 81 days. 2 1/2 months. Pancreatic cancer patients get to live longer than that. I want to show you her videos. I want you

to feel my pain. I want you to stop laughing and continuing
on with your life as if nothing significant has occurred. I don't
want you here. I don't want to talk about her. I do. I don't. I
do. I don't. Yes. No. Yes. No. Rage. It's too hard. I'm exhausted.

I want you to crawl down in this pit with me.

January, 2011

*Every day I try so hard not to fall apart and become stronger
and better. Yet there are so many days when I am in such
despair that I think my mind is going to go someplace really
dark and cold and it will never come back. Some days I want
that. I really do want to die. I have no fear of dying. My
daughter showed me how to do it. I need to go wherever she is
and make sure she's not alone and that she's o.k. and happy. I
need to see her. I need to touch her. I need to hear her laughter.
I need her wisdom. I need to enjoy her sense of humor and
laugh again. I need to watch her perform. I need to tickle her
back. I need to go buy a new pair of shoes with her. I need to
get my daughters together and have a "girl's day out". I really,
really need to wake up from this nightmare.*

Excerpts from "A Grieving Mother's Journal"

January, 2011

*My relationship with my only surviving daughter is fragile
and completely different now. I want to cling and she wants
distance. I want to take her in my arms and keep her so close
to me that she melts into my inner most being. She wants
to be removed. I see her pain. I want to make it go away. I
want to be there for her but she doesn't want me around and I*

understand. I'm too much of a reminder. See looks at me and sees a mirror. A reflection of her loss, too. She looks at me and sees what a lonesome, hard road she has ahead of her. Where's her sister? Her sister should be here to share in the future of her nephew who absolutely adores her. She should be here to watch him go on his first date, get his driver's license, graduate from high school and become a mature adult. Her sister should be here to help her figure out what to do with their aging parents? Now that her sister's gone, who's going to support and help her when I die? Who's going to help her get through another loss even if the next one isn't as devastating? I don't know what to say. I don't know what to do. I don't know the answers. I don't know how to help.

They say one of the steps when dealing with grief is blaming or trying to bargain with God. I never thought I did. I had just decided our relationship was not what I thought it was. Maybe the word was "indifference". All I know is I didn't want to have anything to do with God. However, looking at my journal now, it has all the markings of a person angry, blaming and bargaining.

Excerpts from "A Grieving Mother's Journal"

February, 2011

Very bad days. I can't stop with the guilt and I can't stop seeing and hearing Amy during those last few horrible days of her life. I wonder if God is punishing me for my past sins. I guess I really didn't deserve someone as wonderful as her. I can't stop thinking about all the mistakes I made as a person and a mother.

Excerpts from "A Grieving Mother's Journal"

March, 2011

Today is my birthday and I am 62 years old. Last night Sarah, Jake, Ed and I went to dinner and then to see an amazing concert. It was the Indianapolis Symphony Orchestra with special guest Idina Menzel. It was so creative and thoughtful of Sarah to pull this together for me. I know it was hard for her. Amy was always the planner and Sarah has had to pick up that chore. I am so blessed to have her and Jake and Ed. Today, however, my grief over rides my blessings and I hate that. I've always been able to see blessings first and the down side of life second. But I have never had this intense down side in the 62 years I have been alive. Right now it seems like no blessing will ever outweigh Amy's death. I've dealt with financial troubles, my father's death, divorce, remarriage, kids, step-kids, husband's three open heart surgeries, multiple stents, additional surgeries, mother's cancer and fall, mother's death, loss of jobs, moving and more.....and yet, none of that compares. I am depressed and extremely tearful. Not only for the loss of my daughter, but for the loss of joy.

March, 2011

We're home from my brother's wedding. It was a lovely ceremony and both Tom and Marilyn looked so happy. Ed, Sarah and Jake were there, too. We handled it much better than I thought we would. A ceremony without Amy.

Now that we're home, all I want to do is find every picture of Amy, every musical, every letter, every note she wrote; anything that has her face, handwriting, touch...whatever. Just as long as it's her. She should have been there. She should be here now.

Oh, God. Not another day without her. Not another special event with this huge pain and loss. I'm not sure if I can handle much more.

This was the closest I came to praying. I was done.

March, 2011

I've had a really nasty stomach virus. Several days of nausea, vomiting, dry heaves, diarrhea and headaches. Know what I was thinking during all this? I thought about the days Amy was so sick and how badly her head hurt and the suffering she endured. My little bout of sickness doesn't compare to what Amy went through.

I don't want spring to come. It just means there's another season without Amy. I'm angry. I'm mad at everyone and everything. I can't find a good place to put this rage much less the pain in my heart.

Julia Watson

Excerpts from "A Grieving Mother's Journal"

April, 2011

Does God love someone else more than Amy? Is another person's life more important than Amy's? Is someone, other than Amy, so special that God heals or saves them and ignores our cries? Is there another mother, sister, nephew, husband or friend who deserves answered prayers more than us? I don't know too many people who have touched others more than Amy or has been more of a friend to others than Amy. I don't know too many people who have more to offer through their talents, humor or love of life than Amy. Amy had just as many prayer warriors who were asking for her healing and/ or remission as anyone else facing illness and death. With all that, was Amy's life so less important that God didn't feel the need to answer our prayers and let her live?

So death isn't a big deal to God? Maybe for Him, it's just a very insignificant event. Maybe the only death that really matters to God is the death of Jesus Christ. As for the rest of us, what happens, happens. Cancer, illness, accidents, tsunamis, evil people, and other natural disasters show me how, when it comes to death, God rarely intervenes. The people who survive are no more deserving to live than the thousands who didn't. I get really upset now when people say it was God who saved them or God is healing them or God provided the organ donor or God provided the right chemotherapy for them. Nope. It was just your lucky day. God had other things to do. Telling me that God saved your loved one is like telling me Amy wasn't worth saving.

April, 2011

Seven months and you still haven't come back. Seven months and I'm waking from this nightmare only to find it's not a dream. It's real. Seven months and your sister misses you more and more every day. Seven months and I still keep listening for you. Seven months and nothing has gone back to normal. Seven months and it's still the most unbelievable and devastating experience of my life. Seven months and it's even rawer than the first day you left. Now, seven months later, I can barely look at your pictures or see any reminders of you. My tears are uncontrollable and I don't want to go to bed. I don't want to think about waking up to another day without you in our lives.

Excerpts from "A Grieving Mother's Journal"

May, 2011 (Mother's day)

Painful. Unimaginable. Unspeakable. Uncontainable. Unbelievable. Heart wrenching. Sickening.

Excerpts from "A Grieving Mother's Journal"

June, 2011

I went to Owensboro and found a blessed relief with my long-time friend, Sally. It seems as if she's been my constant during these months. "Bring your videos of Amy. I would love to see them. I think I would like to watch her memorial service again. It was an incredible tribute. I was amazed at what Sarah said and how she held herself together so bravely." What sweet music to my ears. I took the music video (not the service), and what was even more exciting, Sally has a very large TV and her sound system is amazing. Watching the video was like Amy being there. Sally kept talking on and on about her talent and I puffed up like the proud mother I am. She talked about her disbelief that Amy was gone. We cried together, laughed and even talked about other things and other people. I can never repay Sally for what she has done for me.

Excerpts from "A Grieving Mother's Journal"

June, 2011

It's another month for birthdays in our world. Marilyn, Dean, Cindy and Daniel celebrate their special day in the month of June. I think it's funny how the word "celebrate" is so far removed from my vocabulary. Cakes, ice cream, cook outs and presents are motions I go through. I do it for them but deep down I could care less. I keep thinking if I continue to take steps toward the things I once loved to do, then I will eventually find that happiness again. I keep thinking that magically, after we get through the first year, everything will be so much better. We'll find out if that is true when a few more months have passed.

I'm considering calling the doctor and getting some medication. I still have horrible anxiety, especially when it's time to go to bed. I can't figure that one out. My nerves are shot, my thoughts are still raging, I cry every day, I have a hard time dealing with people and my body feels lifeless. That's just to name a few of my symptoms. I don't know if it's a normal grieving thing and will go away or if depression and anxiety have completely taken over my entire being. Maybe some of both. I wonder if there is something I can take that allows me to remember but without the pain.

Excerpts from "A Grieving Mother's Journal"

June, 2011

I noticed Dean has stopped wearing his wedding ring.

Excerpts from "A Grieving Mother's Journal"

July, 2011

Sarah brought home a personality test for us to take. We've all done them many times before, but find it amusing as to how accurate they are. When we finished checking out our own personalities, Ed remembered what Amy's results were. When we read the description, it was so Amy. It also said that this personality trait was very rare; something like only 2% of the population. No wonder we miss her so much. She was one in a million. One of those truly rare, exciting, beautiful souls and being without her really does place a black hole in the universe.

I notice Sarah's beginning to say Amy's name more now. She will compare things that are happening now to things that applied to Amy's life or just a quick remembrance of something that Amy said or did. She still stops short of saying too much about her sister or the loss she feels. Sarah knows if the tears start, they may never stop. We touched on what we are going to do September 22, 2011; the one year anniversary. Are we going to run and hide? Are we going to just pretend it's another day and push through it? Are we going to be alone or do we need to be with each other. I know we will grieve in our own way, but how? I already know I am not going to work on that day. I have never been to Crown Hill Cemetery where Amy's memorial is. I don't know if I will ever go.

Excerpts from "A Grieving Mother's Journal"

Ed's 68th birthday is here and I dropped to my lowest point in a long time. All I could do was remember Amy being here last year and lighting the candles on his birthday cake. How we all laughed when Ed said it was his special day and birthdays trump cancer.

Excerpts from "A Grieving Mother's Journal"

August, 2011

It's the first of August and there's going to be a wedding in Kentucky. I've sent back my RSVP, bought and wrapped their gift. Tom and Marilyn will be there and so will Susan. There's a hitch in the plans. The doctor called and Ed has a "spot" on his lung and is scheduled for a pet scan. It will be done at the oncology department in the hospital where Amy went.

I drove to a place where I never wanted to see or enter ever again. I knew exactly where to go and the room where I would wait while Ed had his scan.

A couple of days passed and they called wanting to do a needle biopsy. We once again entered the same hospital where Amy had been admitted and died. Every inch of that place put me in a depressed, sad and anxious state. Not only reliving all the events from our experience with Amy, but the concern for Ed and what the results of his test may show. I came away from that "procedure" tired and emotionally exhausted.

Excerpts from "A Grieving Mother's Journal"

September/October, 2011

Ed has two spots; one in the lung and the other in a lymph node outside the lung. That was totally unexpected. Once I heard the words "lymph node", I completely shut down. I went numb and unable to react either good or bad. I breathed and walked and talked and worked, all with shut down emotions. After the biopsy on the lymph node, we found out it was not cancer. My reaction was void but pretended to feel excited and relieved. Strange how I didn't feel anything. I guess my mind figured there just wasn't too much more that could be thrown at me. For my own survival, everything went on auto pilot. I still am. Next stop is a visit to the surgeon to decide on surgery to remove the spot in the lung. All of this with September 22 looming. Maybe it's a good thing I'm so numb that the big things don't seem to faze me. Only the little day to day irritations.

September/October, 2011

Our visit with the surgeon made our decision easier. He confirmed the spot outside the lung was not cancer but he also said, in his years of experience, what he read in the report from the needle biopsy the nodule inside the lung, was almost certainly cancer. On September 29, they will remove the "spot".

Julia Watson

From My Letter to Amy (One year anniversary of her death)

September 22, 2011

Amy,

What do I say? How do I begin? It was one year ago today when you left. In so many ways it seems like yesterday and so many other ways it seems like an eternity. They say it gets easier, but I haven't exactly found that to be true. There are some days when I actually go a couple of hours without your memory creeping into my mind. You, however, never leave my heart.

We think and speak of you often. Remembering the things you said or did that made us laugh or just shake our heads, saying, "That's Amy". After a year, Amy, it's not just your family that talks about you. It's so many other people who knew and loved you. So many people who miss you. I wonder if you had any idea of how many people you influenced. Good or bad, the people who knew you were affected by your life.

I remember sitting in the hospital beside your bed and you reached out and held my hand and said "I love you, Mom". When you got up to go to the bathroom and I helped you, you turned around and put your arms around me and laid you head on my chest. It is a memory I will never forget and always treasure. As I held you, it was everything I could do not to sob uncontrollably, but I was so afraid of not being strong enough to help you get through this nightmare. Today, I still feel your touch and hear you saying you love me, and now I can, and do, weep uncontrollably.

I so want to believe you are in a wonderful place with peace, beauty, music and love surrounding you. I want to believe you don't miss us like we miss you. I want to believe you are the happiest you have ever been. It's the only thing I can hold on to. Right or wrong. Wishful thinking or totally unrealistic ideals.... I have to cling to that one thread of hope. It's all I've got. It's the only way to survive without you.

So, Amy, enjoy your place of rest and beauty and love. You deserve it. You gave me rest, beauty and love while you were here. It's your turn now.

Forever,

Mom

Excerpts from "A grieving Mother's Journal"

October, 2011

Ed's surgery is over. Home now and there, of course, are the good days and the bad days. Slowly, things seem to be getting better. The follow up visit with the doctor confirmed the diagnosis of cancer, but assured us it was in the early stages and completely removed. Complete recovery will take time, but it will happen even if it looks impossible now.

October, 2011

Early in November, there will be a Watson brother-sister reunion in Brown County. Hopefully, Ed will be feeling much better for that event. Thanksgiving is around the corner and plans are being made. His son from North Carolina will be in Owensboro that weekend and Ed will go to Kentucky. I'm not going, but not sure what I will be doing. Sarah is off work that week and wants to do something. We'll see how that goes. I have absolutely no desire to do anything but go away for the upcoming holidays. It means nothing to me.

It had been a little over a year since learning about Amy's cancer, her suffering, her death and attending her funeral service. God was not good. God didn't give a flip about us. People had prayed. I had believed. So where was the God that had stepped in and brought us through so many other rough times? If he had prepared everything in advance for us to come and live in Indiana just for the opportunity to watch Amy die, then as far as I was concerned, that was one hell of a cruel joke.

Ed kept going to church and had me on everyone's prayer list. I didn't want to be on anyone's prayer list, anywhere near people of faith or church or hear another praise and worship song ever again. Church was not comforting, in fact the first time I entered a church after Amy's death, I had a panic attack. If I tried to talk to my husband about what I was feeling, I felt his answers were almost flippant. There was almost a dismissal of my feelings. I always felt like he was disappointed in me for not having a stronger belief and faith and yet I wondered if his belief and faith would have been so strong if it had been his own daughter and not his stepdaughter that died. All I really wanted was someone to talk to and listen to me and accept where I was at any given moment. I didn't need to discuss God. I needed to discuss Amy. I needed someone to tell me I was not crazy and whatever I felt was real and absolutely acceptable.

Excerpts from "A Grieving Mother's Journal"

November, 2011

When I stop and think about who would come to a holiday gathering at my house, I realize how empty it is. I remember busy holidays, shopping and hardy meals. Almost every year since my girls were born, my house was the center of activity. After eighteen years, there was Ed and Mother, Tom and Marilyn, Sarah, Jake, Amy, Dean and friends. There were many occasions when Ed's kids and the grandkids came to share in the holidays with us. Now, I can't even include Ed in the Thanksgiving holiday, but I really don't care. I just want to be left alone.

November, 2011

Thanksgiving.

Up, down. Up, down. Up, down. Cook, don't cook. Cook, don't cook. Go away, don't go away. Go away, don't go away. So, it's over. We hurt Dean's feelings and made him mad and I am so sorry for that. It's a story within a story and I really don't care to go over it. I will say that even though I feel badly about what happened, our actual Thanksgiving Day was easy and stress free. As it turned out, we cooked a small but very adequate meal, played games, watched football and relaxed as if it was just another day. Not a holiday. Not a holiday without Amy. Just a day.

Julia Watson

Excerpts from "A Grieving Mother's Journal"

December, 2011

So, today is December 12. I've opened this journal a hundred times since the beginning of December and never found the strength to write anything. Even now, I can't get started. Too afraid of the emotions coming out so strong that I will never get back any control. Too afraid of that bitter taste of knowing that Amy's not here and not ever coming back. In so many ways, it's harder now than one year ago. Everything is still as real, raw and painful as it was then and maybe even more. I wrote a letter wishing Amy a happy birthday last year, but haven't found the courage to do it this year for her 41st birthday. Maybe it's because I think about how she's still 39; just like how I always think of her as my little girl.

December, 2011

Christmas day is over. We made it through even with a couple of giggles. But if I recall, it was always when we were reminiscing about something Amy said or did. We took a "family" photo and when I look at it, there's a glaring absence. It was so incomplete, which is exactly how my life feels. I will never be complete again. I will never be a whole person again.

Chapter 3

2012-They lied

"It's a strange time."

Julia Watson

Excerpts from "A Grieving Mother's Journal"

New Year's Day.....2012

I keep thinking about Amy's life. How there was so much inner turmoil and struggles. Her life was not easy. Bad life experiences, less than perfect parents, definitely a mother that didn't have a clue, a divorced family that she never really came to grips with, her own marriage that we all knew teetered on the edge of divorce for years, infertility, finances, weight, health issues, and mostly, how we expected her to be whatever we needed whenever we needed it. Talk about a heavy load to carry. Who did we call when things went sour or we needed help or we needed a laugh or whatever; good or bad. Always, Amy. Even when she only had a couple of weeks to live, she was the one who called the doctors, made the appointments, took care of the insurance situation, drove all over town to get her pain meds when three out of the four pharmacies didn't have her prescription. She had to take her illness and everything that went with it into her own hands because none of us had the strength to do it. During her last day at home, before the trip to the hospital and eventually her death, she was so sick and in so much pain and everyone was asking her what she thought we should do. I remember her looking at us and almost in tears finally saying "will someone please just make the decision for me". "I can't do it anymore". Shame on us. We all failed her in so many ways. If there is one shred of truth in what I once believed, then my only prayer is that my child is finally at peace.

January, 2012

Ed is feeling better. Lungs are clear and the last heart cath shows no signs of blockages. He's keeping busy volunteering for a couple of churches and helping his brother whenever he needs a ride to doctor's appointments. I've noticed with him and other folks; there's a lack of sensitivity concerning my loss. I think everyone's moved passed it and don't even realize that I haven't. The hurt and sadness are as real today as it was September 22, 2010.

The anniversary, birthday and holidays are over and I'm feeling really down. I can't put my finger on it. I don't know why it's so intense now. I am weepy and every thought is about Amy. I miss her so much. I can't heal. The damage is too deep and I'm not sure if it can ever be repaired.

February/March, 2012

They call it the "new norm" for us; life without Amy. There's nothing normal about it. The days just seem to roll into one, each one passing by without purpose or desire. One step forward, twenty tears backwards, and a total disconnect with the life around you.

My birthday has come and gone. It makes me so sad and so very angry to celebrate my birthday when Amy should be the one celebrating birthdays. Not me. Ed, Sarah and Jake did a great job of making my day special and I know how hard it was for them. In the deepest part of my heart, I appreciate and love them so much.

Amy's husband has been offered a position in Florida. He has accepted. I have, unexpectedly, been shaken by this news. It's not necessarily him leaving as much as it is one more piece of Amy's life will be gone.

Julia Watson

Excerpts from "A Grieving Mother's Journal"

April/May, 2012

April is here. The tree we planted in Amy's memory has bloomed once again. Her husband accepted another job and moved to Florida. There was a birthday party for my brother in law's 70th birthday. Ed & I celebrated (?) our 26th wedding anniversary. Good Friday and Easter arrived. Life seems to keep moving past me while I'm standing still.

It is the time of year when Mother's day, Father's day and all the birthdays are just sitting and waiting for my attention. Ugh. Ed thinks I should go to a little social for pizza, talks and games. You must be kidding! It just confirms my belief that most people, including Ed, have moved passed Amy's death and think I should be passed it too; ready to enjoy socializing with others. I am so disappointed in him. I thought of all people, he should just look at me and know that I'm still hanging on by a thread. Maybe I'm a much better actress than I thought or maybe it's because he's a man. Maybe because he's not wearing my shoes.

May, 2012

So it's Mother's Day; my second without Amy. Yesterday, Sarah and I went and had a pedicure. We went to a place we had never been before. I'm not sure if that was accidental or deep down in the recesses of our minds, something we did on purpose. For Mother's Day, Sarah, Amy and I would go to the nail salon as a treat for all of us. It was usually at the same place. The last time Sarah and I went there after Amy's death, they asked about Amy. It knocked the breath out of us. So that's why we avoided our familiar nail salon. If we go somewhere new and different, we can try to overlook that empty chair beside us and pretend it's just another day; nothing unusual.

Excerpts from "A Grieving Mother's Journal"

June, 2012

Disney World; the last time I went, Amy, her husband, Sarah, Jake, Ed and I were there together. It was seven years ago and Jake had just turned five. This year, Sarah, two of my grandsons and I went. It was good. Some memories from our vacation with Amy crept up into our hearts and minds when we least expected it. It always does. Some memories we have of Disney World with Amy were even spoken out loud. They always brought a smile to our faces.

This trip showed us that we can do things that we once did with Amy and still have fun and survive even if she isn't there. We did make a lot of good memories on this vacation, which is what we so desperately needed. I guess this is what most experts would call "healing and moving forward".

June, 2012

We're almost to July and on the 4th, the countdown begins. 81 days of hell.

Excerpts from "A Grieving Mother's Journal"

July, 2012

4th of July (year 2) is here and it's a downward spiral from now until September 22. I think Sarah was surprised by her reaction. Her day was spent doing chores, going out for lunch and then to Wal-Mart. I don't think it registered how significant this day is until she went to sleep. It was then that her memories kicked in and the nightmares began. Evidently, the kind where you wake up sobbing and crying out. According to Sarah, Amy was back and Sarah kept calling to her and begging her to stay. Amy kept saying she had to leave. Sarah said in her dreams, Amy is beautiful. My heart is broken for the loss Sarah has. I have been so fortunate not to dream about Amy. I can't imagine how excruciating and painful it is to have those dreams and then wake up to an even worse nightmare........reality.

I have no control over my feelings and emotions during this 81 day trip. It hits on July 4th and no matter how hard I try, I am an emotional wreck; weepy, so very, very sad. Did you know, even now, I can still feel Amy lying on the couch, on my lap and me rubbing her back? Every thought is about Amy and it is truly a struggle just to get out of bed and face another day. I don't want to be here. I don't want to watch Sarah's pain. I don't want to hear about birthdays. I don't want to talk about work. I don't want to pay a bill. I don't want to go anywhere. I don't want to see anyone. I don't want to clean house, do the laundry or clean a toilet. I don't want to cook another meal. I don't want to brush my hair or get dressed.

I only want my daughter. I want to be whole again.

Excerpts from "A Grieving Mother's Journal"

August, 2012

I'm getting ready for work and blow drying my hair and start crying. Suddenly, I remembered when Amy lost her hair. The picture she sent after shaving her head, and how she told me that she didn't think it would be a big deal; but when it happened, it was. I think that's when it hit her that she really did have cancer and what she was going to have to go through.

I awoke this morning feeling Amy's touch. It was like I was back to that day in the hospital (not the one where she died)....I was just sitting by her bed, saying nothing, and all of a sudden, she took my hand, squeezed it, and said, "I love you, Mom". Later, Ed and Kelly were standing at the end of Amy's bed talking. Amy had to go to the bathroom, so I helped her get up and move around the bed with her IV contraption. She stopped, turned, and walked straight into my arms. We held each other and I kissed that beautiful bald head as I fought back the tears. Today, I can still hear her tell me that she loved me and I can still feel my arms around her. Pulling it together, I went to work and while there, I realized it was August 22. Exactly one month before the 2nd anniversary of Amy's death.

We know, much too well, how quickly life can turn dark and ugly; and we live with that fear every day now. We never expect the sun to shine or anything good in our life and that has made us completely different people. Sometimes I don't even recognize myself.

Excerpts from "A Grieving Mother's Journal"

September, 2012

A month from hell. Maybe not from hell, but in hell. Only 21 more days to go and here we are, again. Watching, holding your hand, kissing you, talking to you, pumping meds, hearing last rites from someone we don't even know, Hospice, nurses, family ......and waiting. Just waiting. Waiting for that last breath. *Waiting for your chest to cease rising and falling. Waiting until every part of your being leaves us.*

There was so much more living for her to do. So much more to see and touch and feel and love and hate and dream. So young. Too soon.

I reread my letter to Amy on the first year of her death.

Excerpts from "A Grieving Mother's Journal"

October, 2012

It's a strange time. The anniversaries and birthdays are over and the holidays haven't kicked in. It's wonderful when you don't have to worry about money, gifts, cooking, family gatherings or travel. In a way, October's almost like a reprieve from life's extra anxieties that occur throughout the year.

But wait. Something's wrong. I can't turn off the faucet of tears coming from my eyes and this constant reliving Amy's life and death. What the hell? What is it? The anniversary of before, during and after her death is over. Birthdays are over. 4th of July is over. I shuffled through all of it. What's going on?

I finally mention it to Sarah and to my surprise; she has been experiencing the same thing. Evidently, Jake, too. And then it was said......fall. The change of seasons. Spring and summer have come and gone along with the business of those days. And now the leaves have suddenly turned beautiful shades of color; there are crisp, cool mornings and light-weight jackets are around our shoulders. And just underneath, without even knowing it, are deep seeded thoughts of dark and dreary days of winter where everything that was warm and sunny and beautiful, has died.

Excerpts from "A Grieving Mother's Journal"

November, 2012

Here we go.

It wasn't until I reread my journal that I realized I was beginning to heal. It's apparent that my entries were less often and I think at some point I even mentioned that. I now understand my journaling was less frequent because things were slowly changing in a positive way but I refused to write or acknowledge it. In my warped state of mind, I believed if I did that I would somehow be betraying Amy, her memory and her life. People would forget her and my greatest fear of all was that I would too. I now know that is simply impossible.

Excerpts from "A Grieving Mother's Journal"

December, 2012

December 12, 2012 Happy Birthday, Amy. Yes, you'll always be my baby.

I light your engraved picture twice a year. The first is on July 4 and it is turned off at the end of the day on September 22. This marks the time we first learned of your illness until the day of your death. The second time I turn it on is your birthday, December 12. It stays on through December 25. It's my stupid way of outwardly remembering and dedicating this time to you.

December, 2012

It's after Christmas and your light is unplugged, everyone has gone home, Jake is headed to South Carolina and Sarah has returned to work. So it should feel like we're getting back to normal, right? Well, no, it doesn't. There's a "let down" feeling and a feeling of "incompleteness". Is that a word? We did it. We even did it better this year than last, but it's like it shouldn't be over yet. Something's not right. I put on my earphones and listened to you sing. I watched your "The Christmas Quilt" video and saw you on the screen. I waited for you. I kept looking out the front door watching for your car to pull into the driveway. But you didn't come home. I looked for you at Sarah's, sitting at the piano, playing and singing Christmas carols. But you weren't there. I even went to church and expected you to come out on stage with the musicians. But you weren't there, either.

Chapter 4

2013-The definition of insanity

"I wish I had that unmovable faith"

Julia Watson

Excerpts for "A Grieving Mother's Journal"

January, 2013

It's the New Year with all its promises of new beginnings, better health and positive outlooks. Really? OK. This year, I will look for the positive in everything and begin the process of getting out of myself and do some kind of community service. There. I'm done.

I don't feel the urgency to write and bare my soul on paper like I once did. I wonder if that's a sign of healing. Maybe so; or maybe it's just insanity. You know; doing the same thing over and over and expecting a different outcome. It will be three years in September. No matter how often I sit at the computer and vomit up my guts, the outcome is always the same. Amy died. Amy is gone forever. I will never see or touch Amy again. It's such a harsh reality.

February, 2013

It's so cold in Noblesville, Indiana. The winter has been harsh with snow, ice and that stinging on your face from subzero winds. Yuk. I often look out from our back door to make sure your memorial tree is still standing and not harmed by the weather. I so very much want it to grow and flourish. I keep looking for some type of special plaque to place under the tree. It has to be just right. Nothing gaudy and certainly not angels! You hated getting gifts with heavenly angels on them, although some people would say you're now one. How about that? Ironic, isn't it.

Easter, 2013

I have finally come to grips with the realization that God did not kill you. He did not save you either; but he didn't save the 34 year old mother of a toddler who died from breast cancer, and he didn't save those beautiful babies that were gunned down at the elementary school in Newtown, or the nut job that went into the theater and killed people just for the fun of it, and so many other innocent lives. There is no answer to "why". I've known moms and dads who have lost children and people who have lost parents, brothers and sisters. What made me think I was immune to such grief? Was I so arrogant that I believed tragedy was only for others and never me? Oh, I would say things like "there but for the grace of God go I" and "it could happen to me". But I didn't believe it. Deep inside I thought I would never have to bare this burden. It was for others. Never me.

They say the last step in the grieving process is "acceptance". I may be getting close. I will never accept Amy's death, but I will acknowledge her absence and understand that she is gone and will not be back. It doesn't lessen my sadness and emptiness and there are still so many days when my tears flow without warning. I still want her here every minute of every day; but I am better. I think that's true just from my entries in this journal. They are less often. It's been 2 ½ years. I still dread Mother's Day, 4th of July, Sept. 22, December 12 and Christmas. Those are hard days, but the time in between is better.

Julia Watson

Excerpts from "A Grieving Mother's Journal"

May, 2013

Mother's Day

Saturday, Sarah and I went to have our hair done, eat lunch and of course, on our way home, stop by Longs for donuts. Ed and Jake went shopping. Thank God for Ed! Doing our thing before Mother's Day has become a small ritual for us. It's good, but even now, while at the beauty shop where Amy introduced us to the beautician, we always feel her absence and without saying it, miss her so much. Today, for Mother's Day, we will keep it low-keyed with lunch and a movie. How does a mother who gave birth to two daughters, took care of them, bathed, fed, kissed, loved and watched them grow to strong wonderful women, end up on mother's day with only one? Something like that just doesn't make any sense to me.

Excerpts from "A Grieving Mother's Journal"

July, 2013

I miss you terribly and I am amazed that even now after almost three years, the pain is so intense that I'm not sure I can take another breath. There are times when I'm not really thinking of you and suddenly, it will hit me like a huge boulder. You really aren't here; you really did die. It snaps my head back with such a force of reality. All of it so sudden and out of the clear blue.

Excerpts from "A Grieving Mother's Journal"

July, 2013

The car turned left. On the right was the hospital where Amy died; on the left the cancer center. So once again we turned left, went in, got on the elevator and up to the second floor. Turn right and enter into the office on the left. There's an impressive list of specialists names and letters after their name on the window beside the door. Sitting in the waiting room, you can see where the small lab is and to the left is where you go for your chemo treatments. Straight ahead is where you meet with the oncologist who will tell you in a vague way, how everything is looking better. This was my latest trip with Ed.

While waiting, I noticed a family huddled in the corner of the waiting room. Obviously, it was mom, dad and three adult sons and their first visit. They were making small talk, but I could tell that's all it was. Nerves and fear prevented them from really speaking out loud what was really on their minds. Closing my eyes, and in my mind, I can hear all the conversations from her sons and their wives, that took place while sitting around the kitchen table; and all out of mom's hearing distance. "How bad is it?" "Do you think mom can handle it if it involves surgery and chemo?" "What about dad?" "You know he's no spring chicken either". On and on they would ramble and question.

When mom's name was called, they all stood. One of the sons with a clip board and the other with a yellow legal pad. Armed and ready to take notes and make decisions that will change their entire lives forever. Everyone scared. Everyone in disbelief. Everyone wanting to make it go away. Everyone wanting to protect and shield mom from this horrible disease and everything that goes with it. And, of course, they can't. It's not possible.

Excerpts from "A Grieving Mother's Journal"

August, 2013

I can't put my finger on it, but I feel like I've regressed. I'm having a hard time even getting out of bed or wanting to do anything other than stare at a blank wall, eat or sleep. I wish I knew what the trigger has been. It's not September yet, which is an absolute trigger. Maybe it's that Dean has been here for a visit or maybe it's Jake becoming a talented musician. Knowing how much Amy would have contributed to this and how much both of them would have shared unforgettable moments together. I can see her at the piano and Jake with guitar in hand playing and singing right along with her. I can imagine how much she would have loved seeing his band play and how he would have beamed just from her presence there. I can see get-togethers and holidays with Amy at the piano, Jake with guitar and Sarah together with them singing and filling up the entire room with beautiful and unforgettable music.

August, 2013

I went to Safe Haven, a support group for parents whose child has died. The facilitator is a beautiful, soft spoken woman who decided, after the death of her daughter, to do something positive with her life. She went back to college, got her degree in psychology and now works as a grief counselor. I always found the setting at this group event a little strange and awkward. Everyone sits in a circle and takes turns introducing themselves, saying their child's name and giving a brief description of how they died. Many times the mom or dad's throat tightens and the sobbing is so intense, all they can do is bow their heads and sit in agony. Parents attending Safe Haven range from those who have faced a child's death only two weeks prior, along with the "experienced" group members who have endured their loss for years. It was this last group that kept reassuring me that the peaks and valleys really never end. It doesn't matter if it's been weeks or years, there are always triggers and setbacks. But with time, the gaps in between are further apart. They also said to make yourself get up and get out of bed. Walking will also help. Someone even mentioned getting a puppy. That will definitely force you to start moving. I don't think I have the strength to do this alone, but maybe I'll give it a try. I know I was doing better and I really want to rebound from this setback.

August, 2013

Yep, the trigger was music. Every time I hear Jake play or think about the "Battle of the Bands" contest, I begin weeping. How very, very obvious Amy's absence is at this time. Sarah and I were able to touch on that subject. She is having the same emotions, so now I understand where this is coming from. What a blast Amy would be having and how proud she would be. The best aunt in the world and the best second mom to Jake. What an amazing influence she would be and how much Jake would have appreciated her talents. It's an incredible loss for all of us.

August, 2013

The Battle of the Bands is over. They came in second and will play again at a later date. Last Sunday Jake's band played at Christ the Savior Church. (This is one of the churches were Amy worked. She and Sarah were heavily involved in the music program there.) What a struggle it was for the mother and sister of Amy as well as the mother and grandmother of Jake to be sitting in the pew along with the congregation and watching Jake in that very familiar setting.

I kept waiting to see Amy on stage. Why is Sarah sitting beside me? She should be coming out on stage with Amy. How did this happen? Jake on stage and not Sarah and Amy?

After the service, Ed said that if it were not for Amy, Jake would never have had that opportunity. He just had to believe Amy was listening in on Jake's performance. I would like to find that belief somewhere down in my soul. I wish I had that unmovable faith.

Excerpts from "A Grieving Mother's Journal"

September 22, 2013

Here we are. Three years later. Wasn't it just yesterday you were starting first grade? Wasn't it just yesterday my wild child was running around causing me such worry and fear? Wasn't it just yesterday your life had become such joy and friendship for so many people? Wasn't it just yesterday that you were playing the piano with friends and family standing all around singing everything from gospel to musicals? Wasn't it just yesterday you were playing guitar hero with Jake and having Wheeza days? Wasn't it just yesterday you were running around and making plans for another adventure? Wasn't it just yesterday when our relationship was at its best? Wasn't it just yesterday when you gave so much time and patience to Ed during one of his obsessions? Wasn't it just yesterday we found the "lump" on your back? Wasn't it just yesterday when I saw the life leaving your body and the doctor saying there was no brain function? Wasn't it just yesterday when there was a beautiful tribute in your honor, but all done without you there? Wasn't it yesterday or was it an eternity ago? The memories are still so very, very fresh but so unreal. The tears are still so very, very present. The hole in my heart and soul seems to grow more and more every day. There doesn't seem to be much healing.

Today, I will turn off your light. I will remove your memorial picture from my Facebook page. I will watch your videos and read the cards of condolences. I will cry. I will want to comfort your sister. I will want to be comforted. I will cry more.

Tomorrow, if I wake up, I will find that you are still gone, but my "special" day of mourning will be behind me. September 23, is my new "new year's day". Not January 1. There will be upcoming Jake "events", Thanksgiving, your birthday, Christmas and Easter. Another new year to pick up the pieces and not move, but carry on.

Excerpts from "A Grieving Mother's Journal"

October, 2013

I saw a picture of your tree right after we had planted it and I compared it to what it looks like today. It is beautifully shaped, full of dark green leaves and has grown significantly. Funny, and a little crazy, but sometimes I go to that tree and touch the leaves and the trunk listening for you. Sometimes, I even will say your name. The tree continues to thrive and grow strong and gets more beautiful every year. I almost relate to that. You were like that in life. I want to believe that you are like that in death. I want to mirror that image.

Chapter 5

2014-Voices

"I walked into that room with much dread and regret"

2014

October, 2013, was my last entry into *"A Grieving Mother's Journal"*. It seemed repetitious to continue writing. Good days, bad day. My life was just on auto-pilot. Nothing really mattered. Holidays and anniversaries came and went. I was either angry, remorseful, restless or sad. There's a song that says, "It must be winter in my heart". Perfect description.

I shuffled through November and December but always with the same dread and sense of loss. Our extended families have divided up into their own little worlds. Holidays are spent separated and I think that may become our "new norm". This winter has been especially harsh. Days and days of subzero temperatures and snow almost every day for weeks and weeks. Never ending grey, dark days. All I really want is to go to a nice warm beach and melt. I honestly believe it would give me strength to move forward. Something different and more relaxing than trying to pretend I'm enjoying myself. Running away, however, is not an option. My loss follows me where ever I go.

Spring. Most days were good. Never great, but I'll take good over what was within me for the last three years. I could actually be around "religious" people/groups without rolling my eyes. I even made it to church one day during the Easter season. It became easier to be around happy people and not have a sense of resentment for their joy. I believe even though we didn't recognize it, we were beginning to see a glimmer of happiness back into our lives. It is undeniable that we will always feel Amy's absence, especially during holidays and life changing events with Jake. Every time Jake sings, plays in the band or pulls some obscure hilarious remark out of his back pocket, we will think about how much Amy would have loved it and how much Jake would have loved having her there. Sometimes we even see a hint of Amy in him. Jake's high school prom, first date and graduation will be a real stressor and all the highlights and adventures in his life will renew our sense of loss. I know that and will have to face it head-on.

No more journal entries.

Friday, June 19, 2014

My husband had gone to a meeting and I was at home, trying to decide what I wanted to do. My sister-in-law was coming for an overnight visit on Saturday so I really should clean the bathrooms and scour the toilets. If there's anything in the pantry, I could whip up some snacks? Oh no, that would require a trip to the grocery. No way. Maybe I'll just check out my email and sign in to Facebook. There's always such interesting news on social media and recipes that I will never need or use. I have a site on ancestry.com. I can look up where my great-great-great grandparents lived and died. Of all these exciting choices, I did what I knew had to be done; cleaning and straightening up the house.

As you have read from my previous rantings; God, Jesus, Heaven and life without Amy were a rotating, invading, and questioning constant in my brain. People prayed. I tried church a couple of times. I even went so far as having a church small group in our home. I tried talking to my husband but found it impossible to share with him. Several times I picked up the Bible that Amy, Dean, Sarah and Jake had given me. I placed it back on the shelf without opening it. Everything I thought I believed about God and His love and His power had been shaken and placed in doubt after Amy's death. Yet, I couldn't stop. I just needed to know that my precious child was alive, happy, healthy and safe. I really didn't care about myself. Just her. I needed to talk to someone but could never find that person or the words to say.

Now, back to Friday. I've cleaned the bathrooms and kitchen. Dusted. Washed, dried and changed the sheets on the beds. And then, for some nonsensical reason, looked into the office. You have to understand about the office. Three bookcases containing books, albums, pictures, cookbooks and other knick knacks, two desks and a work table fill that small room. There are boxes on the floor with my unfinished projects, file cabinets and a mound of music cd's that either have or have not been loaded onto iTunes. Honestly, the bookcases haven't been dusted in.....well, let's just say, for quite some time.

I walked into that room with much dread and regret. I knew once I started cleaning, it would take hours to complete this project but decided to forge ahead. I thought I might even rearrange and toss out old, outdated books, even an old Joyce Meyer Bible I had acquired back in the days of belief. So I picked up my dust cloth and began.

It happened on the very first shelf. I picked up a stack of small books that had been strategically arranged on their side just as I had seen on all the HGTV decorating shows. Suddenly, I looked down and the book I held was titled "Prayers from a Nonbeliever". I opened it, and there, hand written on the inside cover was, *"Merry Christmas!" "Love, Amy"*.

You will never know or understand the enormous impact that little book had on me that Friday morning. The overwhelming presence of Amy and God filled my entire being. From Amy's very own lips, I could hear her speaking that old, familiar saying she had repeated so many times before; *"It's all good"*. She was fine and above all, there was hope. Not necessarily complete understanding, but hope. After my sobbing, praying, thanking and asking for forgiveness; there was something I had not experienced in almost four years - peace. My child and our God spoke to me. Totally unexpected and unprepared. But they did. They told me you can grieve and have sorrow, but there is more. There is hope and peace from a God that loves us. It was truly, Amazing Grace.

Now, it's time to figure out what's next. To be truthful, I will have to ease back in to this. Opening a Bible, singing praise and worship songs, and attending church have not been welcoming or soothing for me. But now, one thing for sure, whenever I think back to that Friday and to my dusty, cluttered, overcrowded little home office, I will find myself with a peaceful heart and a grin on my face.

Julia Watson

June, 2014

Interesting things have started moving in and around me.

I can't believe it happened but on Sunday, I went to church by myself.

I picked up Amy's Bible and saw where she had hand written, "1 Thessalonians 5:12-24" and "Romans 8:28" *(And we know that in all things God works for the good of those who love him...)* I, of course, read and reread those passages.

I downloaded a praise song on my iTunes.

I ordered a book about God's grace on my Kindle.

There is a woman at work who has been so sad and troubled and the other night I found myself wanting to hold her hand and pray with her. Lord, help me on that one! I never wanted to do something like that even on my best "believing" days.

Instead of never expecting anything good or just moving through the motions, I'm saying 'what next?' And I'm saying it without sad and depressed thoughts. I'm saying it with hopeful expectations. The assurance of knowing I'm not alone and in spite of the rough times, there is a bigger picture.

Maybe, in some ways, an abstract picture. But that's ok. Right now, I just know that it's one of those pictures you may not totally understand but everyone agrees it is truly a beautiful painting. I know every day will not be filled with special divine and inspiring moments but if I start to lose my perspective, all I have to do is look back to Friday, June 19, 2014.

I wrote this story in early 2008 while doing the "Starting Pointe" series at church. It was written almost three years prior to Amy's death. The purpose was to tell the group what event or events had effected you so drastically that you were changed spiritually. At that time, I didn't feel there was any inspiring story for me to tell. Something, however, moved me to write it. Now when I read this little story, I find it amazing how relevant it is today.

The Watch

Several years ago, I noticed my arms were getting shorter and the face on my watch getting blurrier and harder to read. So I went on a mission to find what I needed. For two or three months, I looked through the "watch" section at all the department stores, discount stores and even your local pharmacy. Finally, I found the perfect watch that fit my needs exactly. I could actually see the numbers without my glasses; it wasn't so large and bulky that it looked like I was trying to change my gender and it was fashionable enough that I could wear it with almost anything. It was also a watch that was dependable and no matter how many times I banged it against something, dropped it or accidentally got it wet, it continued to work.

A couple of years ago, we went on vacation to South Carolina and Cumberland Falls. After being home a few days, I was getting ready to go to the grocery and couldn't find my watch anywhere. I asked everyone at home if they had seen it. The answer was no. I looked in all the obvious places, but it wasn't there. I pulled the suitcases down from the closet and searched in every crack and crevice and still, no watch. I emptied and shook out every purse in my possession and still, no watch. I turned coats, jackets and pants upside down and still, no watch. I checked my make-up bag, jewelry box, glove compartment and trunk of the car and still, no watch. My watch was gone. I bought a cheap replacement, but still found myself occasionally looking in odd places for my old one but knew after all that time, it probably wasn't going to be found.

Two weeks ago, I pulled out an old pair of shoes from the back of my closet and found my watch tucked neatly down in the toe of the shoe. After two years, I had found my watch. You can't imagine how excited, relieved and surprised I was to find it. It was like getting together with an old, reliable friend. I couldn't wait to tell my husband and daughter about my find.

Then, I heard a little voice inside my head saying, "Here's your story". You see, just a couple of days prior to these events I had told my husband I didn't have a story to share with our group. There was no heart surgery or life threatening injury that caused me to reach out to God in desperation or for calmness and reassurance. It was just me doing life the only way I knew how. And yet, here, all of a sudden, I was holding my story in my hand and felt it deep in my heart.

That day, I understood; even though I couldn't see it, just like my watch, my Savior had always been there; never far away and waiting to be found. Something I could depend on, toss in a shoe, bang against a wall, drop in water, wear with everything and see, even without my glasses. Like my watch, God had been there all along. I was just looking in all the wrong places. All I need to do (just like my watch) is put Him on, wear Him and never take for granted His dependability and simple beauty. My watch needs to have the batteries recharged when it starts to lose its energy and so do I. I get recharged by attending church, bible study, sharing life with my family and doing life with my small group. There are cheap imitations, but none of them come with a lifetime guarantee. My watch story is my Lord's story and I will never look at it the same way again.

July 4, 2014

Today I will turn on the plaque with your etched picture on it and it will stay on until September 22. That has become my tradition to remember and honor you. It stays lit from the time we found out you had cancer until the day your light here on earth went out.

I miss you so much and I am sad but for the first time in four years, not in despair.

"Now is your time of grief, but I will see you again and you will rejoice, and no one will take away your joy." John 16:22 NIV

Epilogue

Amy's Christmas Note

Julia Watson

Spire, Greenwood UMC newsletter

December 99   **Music Notes**

Do you remember music throughout your life? Does recalling a certain song bring you to a certain place in time? My favorite memory is of Elvis. Yes, I know, Elvis is an unlikely candidate for one of my greatest memories. (I promise not to make any references to Elvis being "before my time".) Ha! Ha!

I was blessed by God with parents who adored all kinds of music. I am so grateful for that. Their instillation of music in my life has greatly affected every path I chose and every joy or sorrow I encountered. My mom played the piano, my dad played piano by ear and played the trumpet, and they respected and truly enjoyed a vast array of musical genres. In my parents record album collection lived Neil Diamond, Willie Nelson, Mozart, Mahler, BB King, Dan Fohgelberg, the Eagles (from whom I learned harmony at an early age), Barbara Streisand, operas, musicals, symphonies, rock and roll, jazz, blues, country and the list went on. With every album I made new memories. Elvis was one of them.

On a Saturday morning during each Christmas season, Mom would haul out the Christmas decorations, wake Sarah (my little sister) and I up early and we would start our yearly decorating extravaganza. The Christmas album of choice was Elvis' 'Blue Christmas'. Mom, Sarah and I would sing together all kinds of Christmas songs all day. I don't know if you remember, but when Elvis sings "I'll have a Blue...." the backup singers howl "Ooh, ooh, ooh, ooh, ooh...." and the three of us were particularly grand with that part. Whenever I hear that song I can smell pumpkin bread, cookies and a fresh cut tree. I can feel the glass Christmas ornaments in my hand and pine needles painfully punching through my bare feet. I can remember choosing (or should I say arguing) with my sister about which side of the tree Santa would put our gifts. But most of all, I feel safety, love and joy.

Christmas is not the same without the classics of carols, and of course, the classic of Elvis and others. But it is especially not the same without family and friends. So this Christmas include music in your memory-making. Jan Anglund said that "A bird doesn't sing because he has an answer-he sings because he has a song". Sing the song of Christmas and Jesus' birth. Sing the song of love, caring, reconciliation, joy and hope. Sing the song of "Peace on Earth and Good Will to Men".

-Amy

Amy K Reynolds

December 12, 1970 – September 22, 2010